Psalms In The Sand

TRACEY BASSETT-DAVIS

Copyright © 2021 Tracey Basset-Davis

All rights reserved, including the right of reproduction in whole or in part in any form. No part of this publication may be stored in any retrieval system or transmitted in any form or by electronic, mechanical, photocopying, recording, or otherwise without the publisher's written permission. Scriptures marked KJV are taken from the KING JAMES VERSION (KJV): KING JAMES VERSION, public domain.

Manufactured & printed in the United States of America

ISBN: 978-0-578-35846-8

Publisher Tracey Bassett-Davis

Publishing Consultant

For inquiries and speaking engagements, contact Tracey Bassett-Davis at born2worshiphimenterprises@gmail.com

PSALMS IN THE SAND

This book is dedicated 1st to my Heavenly Father, who showed me how to give Him praise through His Word. To my husband, Pastor Mark A. Davis, if it weren't for your heart to see me succeed, this book would not be in existence. My children Jeremy, Devon, Mark Jr., Christine, and Naomi, I love you all to life for real. To Pastor Orlando Ray Hill and my best friend Bertha Phillips, who have gone on to be with the Lord. I am forever grateful to God for allowing these two to be used as important points of contact for me to be freed from a bondage I didn't even know I was in. To my Founding Senior Pastors Roosevelt and First Lady LaFonda Bradley from Life Church International. Thank you for always giving examples of how to be the best I can be and helping me see the result of what can be done with faith, corresponding action, and persistence. The purpose of this book is to show you how to get into the presence of God effectively by using the scriptures found in the book of Psalms. Welcome to the wonderful world of authentic praise and worship through the Word of God!

Table of Contents

Knowing God 1
"Sing Unto God, Sing Praises To His Name"… Ps. 68:4 14
Entering His Gates With Thanksgiving 17
Entering His Courts With Praise/Singing Your Song to the Lord 19
Let's Enter His Gates Together… 21
Let's Enter His Courts With Praise… 24
More Gems To Help Worship Him In Spirit And Truth. 28
Conclusion 29
About The Author 33

Knowing God

The first step towards getting into the presence of God is dependent upon you having a personal relationship with Him. John 10:27-28 says, *"My sheep hear my voice, and I know them, and they follow me: And I give unto them eternal life, and they shall never perish, neither shall any man pluck them out of my hand."* I have learned during my true walk with the Lord that knowing of Him and actually knowing Him are two entirely different things.

Matthew 7:21-23 says, *"Not everyone that saith unto me Lord, Lord, shall enter into the kingdom of heaven but he that doeth the will of my Father which is in heaven. Many will say to me in that day, Lord, Lord, have we not prophesied in thy name? And in thy name cast out devils? And in thy name done many wonderful works? And then I will profess unto them, I never knew you depart from me, ye that work iniquity."* When you have an authentic or real relationship with God, you know Him, and He knows you. Going to church every Sunday or whatever day you go to church is not enough; serving in church isn't enough either. As you can see in the scripture, we just read his response to those who served. It's all about having a personal relationship with God PERIOD.

Let me share who I am and about the journey that catapulted me into an encounter with God that has truly changed my life forever. My mother used to embarrass me by telling everyone she could about the story of yours truly being an infant in her arms while sitting in her favorite rocking chair in the nursery of our house. She would say that I would always have my hands clenched shut, and one day, while she was stroking my hands open, she noticed I had very long, thin fingers. She said the Holy Spirit whispered into her ear, *"She has Piano hands."* As I grew, sure enough, I started tinkering around with the piano at the tender age of 3 years old. I was playing music by ear and started taking piano lessons from 5th to 8th grade.

I had never had a real encounter with the Lord until I was good and grown with two sons that I love dearly out of wedlock on my side. I've been in church all my life and was raised a Seventh-Day Adventist; I was a sure-nuff church girl. Let me say I love all of my brothers and sisters of the SDA faith. You will always have a special place in my heart. I learned a lot back then that makes much sense now, so I praise God for every teaching I was exposed to while growing up. Back then, when I became an older teen, I knew how to be the *"church girl"* and the girl around the way as soon as church got out. When I grew up and got on my own, I was the one drinking communion juice once a month but drinking the devil's juice every day, getting buzzed and high with my cool but worldly friends. Before I connected with the world, I made a serious attempt to fit in with the young people at the church that I thought was cool. I wanted to feel accepted and be normal like the other kids. There were some kids my age whom I made a semi-connection with, but it was only an at-the-church situation. With my mother being a Sabbath School Teacher and First Woman Elder, I was the youngest pianist they had at the church during that time. Thank you, Elder Sandra Turner and Sister Carolyn Kennedy-Hampton. I will always look up to you both as mentors and examples of musical excellence. You gave me courage and a chance to flow in my childhood gift; for that, I give you all honor. I had to say that quickly and give them their flowers because I have to give honor to whom honor is due right? Okay, getting back to my testimony. So, when I tried to be friends with others, it was somewhat challenging. It was like, "Oh, that's Elder Bassett's daughter. She holier than thou, so we don't wanna hang out with her." I'm not 100% sure if that was the case, but that's how I felt.

We lived in another city and traveled daily to where we went to church, so it was awkward for me to connect with others regularly because of the distance in which we all lived. I had always been the weird one trying too hard to fit in. Don't get me wrong, there were a few friendly kids from that time I grew up with that treated me okay. They were probably the ones that would have made my pre-teen life a little bearable. But just like any other pre-teen still trying to find themselves, I wanted to hang out with the "In Crowd." So, I began to extend myself to those I thought were my friends who were really popular, only to be crushed by the realization that they were talking about me behind my back and weren't my friends at all. Do you know what the kicker in that was? They only hung out with me because I could play the piano, and they got close because they wanted me to play the piano for them. I got over it, but as soon as I was 18 years old, I transferred my membership to another SDA Church in another state and continued to live my life. The last straw for me and the church was when I got pregnant out of wedlock and was sat down from doing one of the things I loved most other than playing the piano, which was singing in the choir. I didn't get any counseling. No one took me by the hand to encourage me. I was just told I was no longer a good example to any other young people and that I could no longer be a part of the music ministry until I was deemed ok to return. That was it. I was heartbroken, condemned, unloved, abandoned, uncared for, and pushed to the side. Yeah, that's a lot, but that's how I felt during that time.

Even though I was hurting, I was determined to press my way to church every Sabbath; I just decided to sit in the back of the church so no one could see me, and I even went to the extreme of leaving the service just before church dismissed not to allow any of the other young people to witness the state I was in. Even then, I could still feel the churchgoers' stares as I left the building. One day, I couldn't take it anymore and told myself I would never go back, and I didn't. I kept the denominational practices and decided to stop attending church. After all, who would miss a single unwedded mother anyway?

As time passed, I decided after having my first son to take a class and get my CNA Certificate. About a year later, I got a job as a Nursing Assistant in a skilled nursing facility. The first week of working there was interesting for me. One day, while on my break, I heard two women's named, Bertha Phillips and Stephanie Harris, singing "I've Decided to Make Jesus My Choice." There was a piano in the room where they were, so I sat down and played and added my tenor voice to their Soprano and Alto, and the group Sounds of Revelations was born.

We went on as a group to do many things. We recorded, wrote, and arranged music together and even had an opportunity to be the opening ministry for a concert where Yolanda Adam was the guest artist in Battle Creek, Michigan. At that time, even though I was not going to an SDA Church, I still followed most denominational beliefs. Eventually, I started fading from that and eased into getting more worldly. I began to curse, drink, and smoke cigarettes and Marijuana. By this time, I was playing for 1st Day Sunday Churches and getting paid to play keyboard or piano and to choir direct. This was icing on the cake for me because I was getting paid for what I loved to do.

Bertha and I had become best friends and eventually began studying God's Word on her front porch. Now, mind you, I said I was born into the Seventh Day Adventist faith. It's all I knew. So, even in a backslidden condition, I was still holding on and honoring some of my denominational upbringings. One day, Bertha told me, "You know the Word of God tells you not to allow any man to tell you what day to go to church on, right?" I replied. "No, it doesn't, Bertha! If it does, you have to show me where it's at and give me the book, chapter, and verse it's found in. I'm from Missouri, the show me state, you gotta show me!" She just shook her head and laughed.

The next time we got together to do another outside on her porch Bible Study, she asked me the same question. I gave her the same reply, only this time she backed it up with a scripture from Colossians 2:16 & 17 that read, *"Let no man therefore judge you in meat, or drink, or in respect of an holyday, or of the new moon, or of the Sabbath Days which are a shadow of the things to come; but the body is of Christ."*

Needless to say, after she read that scripture, I was instantly delivered, at least from that bondage, and that evening marked the beginning of my road to an encounter with God. As time passed, I began to read the Word of God on my own. I wanted to learn how to read the King James Version since that was the version I grew up with. There are so many versions of the Bible out there, and more times than not, they have watered down the gospel and turned it into something God had not intended. So, I wanted to stick with the version I grew up reading. My only issue was I could not understand it.

So one day, after griping Bertha about it, she told me to ask God to give me an understanding of the King James Version of the Bible; I did, and He answered my prayer without me even realizing it. I had a full-blown argument with Bertha one day concerning what version of the Bible she had given me to read while at her house for Bible Study. She finally said, "GIRL, God done, answered your prayer!" Listen, I am a living witness that when you ask in faith, God hears and answers us when we pray. I'm a living testament to that.

As I began to grow and mature in the things of God, I never knew that God was tangible (touchable). I always pictured Him as some faraway character in a book with old stories that weren't relatable. But as I grew in God, He revealed Himself to me through His Word. My very first encounter with Him was as a deliverer. As I shared earlier, I used to smoke, drink, and do other things in life that I already knew were contrary to God's Will for me.

As I began down my road to transformation, the Holy Spirit began dealing with me concerning the smoking habit that I acquired while trying to be cool with others. I never bought a carton of cigarettes because I knew that would open the door for big issues, so I was somewhat disciplined in that area; I would only purchase three packs of cigarettes a week and then buy three more when needed. I was a singer and began noticing that smoking was affecting my voice. I had smoker's breath all the time, and quite frankly, I was growing weary of spending the money to keep the habit up.

One hot Saturday Night in July, after a singing engagement with the group we were a part of. Bertha and I left for an outdoor tent revival in East Chicago, Indiana; it seemed like everything that could go wrong did. It was like the devil himself did not want us to get there. I had never in my life experienced as much drama trying to get to a place as I did that evening. While we were going there, I had an open and frank discussion with God. I gave Him an ultimatum because, by this time, I had been sick and tired of being sick and tired of smoking. So I told God in front of my best friend, "God, if you don't deliver me tonight from smoking, I'm going to leave right after service to a gas station to buy a carton, and I will be a human smoke stack!" Mind you, I said this while I was smoking the last cigarette I had on me from the three packs I purchased earlier in the week.

Bertha looked at me and said, "Ooooooh, you just challenged God!" I looked at her and said, "I guess I did; I'm sick and tired of doing this, now either He is going to take this smoking away, or I'm going to go and get the carton of cigarettes." I said. I'd never get and become a human smokestack after service over tonight! We got to the tent revival and sat under it; it was one of the hottest summer evenings. I remember sitting there with my friend, listening to this traveling evangelist preach about miracles, signs, and wonders and how God is a healer. Bertha nudged me and said, "Tracey, I had a dream about this. I kid you not! No wonder the devil tried to keep us from getting here. Something good is about to happen tonight."

I looked at her like a deer caught in headlights because, inside my heart, I felt anxious and excited, feeling that something was about to change. Come to find out that the speaker was a well-known traveling evangelist with a healing ministry who has been all over the United States. He had a gentleman with him who survived being shot almost fatally and had the X-rays to prove just what God did to spare his life.

The testimony was truly a miraculous one. I latched on to every word spoken that night in the tent. When it was time for the altar call, the

Evangelist asked for anyone with addictions to come up for prayer. People flooded the front, so I took my queue and got in line with the others. When it was my turn to be prayed for, the Evangelist looked me right in the eye and said, "You know what you need to do for God, young lady, right?"

All I could do was nod yes as if I fully understood what he meant (I didn't). I was scared. I couldn't even speak, and why was I crying so profusely and shaking? I thought to myself. Now, mind you. I had never been to a church service like this one in all my life. I had never had anyone "Lay hands" on me, and neither have I ever fallen out under the Power of God. "Do what He tells you to do!" said the traveling preacher as he reached out and put his hand on the top of my head. I felt something like a jolt of electricity go through my body, and then I fell to the ground backward. I think the people behind me broke my fall to the ground. I didn't care who saw me or who didn't because, at that point, I was having my first real connection with God.

I stayed down there on the dirt floor of that tent for what seemed to be like 10 minutes, shaking and crying. When I finally got up off the floor, I went back to my seat, looked at my friend who was watching over me the whole time, and said, "Mhmm, I bet you got what you challenged God for tonight!" I was still crying at this point and felt God all over me. I told her, "You know what? I think you're right. I don't even want a cigarette right now…"

Bertha drove me home. I got in the house, readied myself for bed, and started thinking about that evening's events. I still felt "tipsy and tingly" from my first encounter with the Lord at the tent revival. I could still feel God's Presence on me, so before I went to bed, I requested that God take control and never leave my presence. The next day, I woke up anticipating feeling the same way I did the night before. I woke up and said, "God, are you here?" And I felt His warmth all over me again. I even went all morning without one cigarette!

I was so excited that I went to my friend's house, whom I used to hang out and "do stuff' with. I shared what had happened to me the night before. I told her I felt different and communicated the testimony of what happened before and during the service. I believed that God had delivered me from smoking and that I accepted the Lord as my personal Savior. She just looked at me and said, "Wow, that's good, Tracey!" I looked at her and said, "Hey, give me one of your squares and a lighter…"

"No, Tracey, you not about to have God mad at me cause you tryin' to backslide already and got me helping you do it." I said, "I just want to see something. I'll be fine. Just give me the cigarette already!" She finally gives in and hands me one. I go on to light it, and she says, "Tracey, you don't even look right with that cigarette in your mouth. You need to stop!"

Well, Men and Women of God, let me be the one to say when I took that first inhale, I almost got sick to my stomach! It tasted horrible; I couldn't even finish it and gave it back to her.

She said, "See, I told you don't be trying God. He done did something for you." I told her she was right, and I ended up repenting to God for testing to see if I was really delivered when I already knew in my heart I was. In my ignorance, He could have allowed me to ease back into that bondage, but His grace and mercy kept me in spite of me.

As time went on I was led to start looking for a church home where I could be nurtured and begin growing and maturing in the things of God. I began to acknowledge Him so He could direct my path due to the talent I used for the church. Of course, the enemy used familiar people to get me into a place for their own gain, and they did it in the Name of Jesus, or so they said. You have to know who you are in Christ and be secure in that thing, own it, and don't let anyone get you off your square. This is the sole reason why you have to test the spirit by the spirit is to make sure what's being told to you is of God. Because just as sure as God has a plan for your life, you better know and believe that the enemy has one too, and he will use anyone to get you sidetracked from the assignment God allowed you to be born to carry out. Let me say this like I feel it: if you are not seeking God for direction and are not using Godly discernment, the enemy will use secular and or church folks who are not where they need to be in God as a pawn to get you out of the Will of God. Bertha and I were both looking for a church to be planted at. She ended up going to a couple of churches, including one where she was raised all her life. I ended up joining one of the 1st Day Churches I played the Piano for because the pastor's wife said God told her that's where I was supposed to be. So, I didn't have peace the day I went to the altar to join the church. I felt very unsettled about it. I tried to talk to the pastor's wife about it after church that day, but she avoided me. It was as if she knew she had done wrong. Longer story short, I quit and formally left that ministry.

Needless to say, I was still looking for a church to be planted in, and so was Bertha. She had a friend named Birda Hill who had married this Church of God in Christ preacher by the name of Orlando Ray Hill (he's gone on to be with the Lord now). She shared that she had been to their church before and loved the service and was thinking about going to one of their weekly Bible Study services and invited me to come with her. I figured, what do I have to lose? So I went.

I remember that phenomenal Tuesday evening encounter with God as if it were yesterday. Bertha picked me up and we went to a house that was turned into a church. There were old movie theater seats that had not been bolted down to the floor on both sides of the small sanctuary that used to be someone's living room. There was an organ at the front of the church, a drum set, and a podium where the preacher gave messages of the Gospel.

We came in and sat down, and joined in with the devotion. At the beginning of the service, we listened to the preacher as he taught us about the love of Jesus and how important it was for us to have the Holy Spirit in our lives. At the end of the service, he opened up the altar for those who wanted to accept the Gift of the Holy Spirit with the evidence of speaking in tongues.

I didn't know what to expect, but I got in that line, ready to receive what God had for me that night. Bertha stood in front of me in line. There were a few more people in front of her. The church pastor began laying hands on people, and they fell onto the floor and began crying. Some talked in tongues. When he laid his hands on Bertha, who was in front of me, she fell out, but then I felt something hot land on top of my head and went straight through me. I fell out onto the floor. The people behind me caught me and carefully guided me to the floor.

I felt like I was on fire. I couldn't speak. Tears were flowing profusely. My mouth was open, and a noise came out that I didn't recognize. I couldn't move. It felt like I was pinned to the floor. I heard the pastor walk by me with tear-filled eyes; I saw him stop briefly before going to the next person in line and saying with a loud voice, "Seal her God until the time of redemption!" I stayed on the floor for approximately 20 minutes when I finally got off. I felt drunk and still felt heat surging throughout my body and a solid, tingly heat in my mouth. Bertha was the same way. That was the night we both received the Gift of the Holy Spirit. It was amazing. We both cried in the car back to the city I lived in. We talked about how we didn't ever want this feeling to end and how wonderful God was. Then we would feel Him all over again and cry more uncontrollably. We stopped at our beloved coffee shop before going home and began with the waterworks again while trying to order our coffee in the drive-thru. I tell you when you want God and His powerful presence to show up at times all you can do is cry because it's a wonderful, overwhelming place to be.

I know the people listening inside the store probably thought we were crazy, but they went on and took our order after we were able to talk. They were waiting for us at the window to ensure we were ok. Bertha told them we had just left Bible Study and had an awesome meeting with God Himself. Of course, they didn't understand. We didn't care at that present moment. All we knew was that we didn't want that feeling to end. Bertha dropped me off at my house. As I got ready for bed, I felt warm and tingly. I remember telling God thank you and to please let me feel the way I do now tomorrow. "Please don't leave me I whispered to Him before falling asleep.

The following day I arose feeling like I woke up from a dream. Remembering it was all real, I felt God's presence all over me the same way I felt Him the evening before. I am extremely grateful to God for the encounter He allowed me to have. I returned to the church and became an active member of the Day of Pentecost Church Of God In Christ the Sunday following Tuesday Night.

I got saved and dedicated myself entirely to learning all I could about God. From that day forward, I started a real relationship with Him, taking me from faith to faith and glory to glory in my Christian Walk. I was so hungry for His presence that I did whatever I could to make that happen through the leading of the Holy Spirit. I read the Bible every day and spent quality time with Him thru prayer and fasting.

All of these things need to be done to have an authentic relationship with God. When I got saved for real (been in church all my life remember?) I never knew or was taught how to get before Him for myself and how important cultivating a personal relationship with God was. After my last encounter with Him, I began to read scriptures that talked about what happens when you get into the presence of God correctly.

"It came even to pass as the trumpeters and singers were as one to make one sound to be heard in praising and thanking the LORD; and when they lifted up their voice with the trumpets and cymbals and instruments of musick, and praised the LORD saying, For he is good, for His mercy endureth for ever; that then the house was filled with a cloud, even the house of the LORD; "so that the priests could not stand to minister by reason of the cloud; for the glory of the LORD had filled the house of God. (2Chronicles 5:13,14.)

Even though this particular scripture talks about what happens when the musicians, priests and singers are all on one accord and everyone is obedient to what God said to do in the corporate setting. Encounters with God are still attainable today just like in the Bible days. Guess what? You too can attain this same atmosphere in the privacy of your own home. I can hear you asking now, "How can I do that? I don't play any musical instruments. I can't even carry a tune in a bucket if I wanted to. How can I set the atmosphere for God to come visit me like that?" In the words of my Senior Pastor Roosevelt Bradley Jr, "I'm glad you asked!"

Start by giving genuine thanks to God verbally. Lord, I thank you for waking me up this morning. Thank you for keeping my family and I safe. Thank you for food to eat, clothes on my back, and a place to live. No one knows but you concerning what He's done for you, so enter in His gates with thanksgiving (Psalms 100:4). When you do this genuinely and sincerely, it will open the door for authentic or "real" praise.

Play some authentic praise and worship music in your home, songs like "Good God" by Benita Jones, "Name Above All Names" by Eddie James, "Lord You Are Good" by Israel and New Breed, and "The Lord is Good" by Fred Hammond are excellent songs of praise to get you into a real moment of ministering to the Lord through praise.

This is the place we are aiming to be, in His presence. Songs like "More Than Anything" by Lamar Campbell, "King of Glory" by Shana Wilson, "My Worship" by Phil Thompson "In" by William McDowell, and "All Hail The King/We Worship You In The Spirit" by Shekina Glory Ministries are specific songs that minister to God Himself and are guaranteed to take you into authentic worship that will guide you into the "Throne Room" or Holy of Holies which is the place where God resides.

Praise and worship is for God, *not for us* it is what draws Him to us (James 4:8). The Bible gives the command for everything that has breath to praise the Lord (Psalms150:6). It also gives us clear direction on what God is expecting from us as His people concerning worship. In John 4:23 - 24

"But the hour cometh, and now is, when the true worshippers shall worship the Father in spirit and in truth; for the father seeketh such to worship him. God is a Spirit: and they that worship him must worship him in spirit and in truth." So there you have it. In order to worship Him you must be in the spirit. Anything outside of that is not true worship. You cannot worship Him if you are in your flesh and worldly-minded. It says in Romans 12:2, *"And be not conformed to this world; but be ye transformed by the renewing of your mind, that ye may prove what is good, and acceptable, and perfect, will of God."*

The Word of God plainly outlines what the Lord is requiring of us concerning getting before Him. When done correctly from a sincere heart and a renewed mind that seeks to please Him, setting up ways to abide in Him by supplying a place for Him to dwell in your home opens up the door for the atmosphere to be set for the miraculous in your life. This book is to be used to help you get into the presence of God through using the scriptures from the Book of Psalms.

When you read the scriptures, use them in the first person to make them personal between you and God. This will open the door to an intimate dialog between you and the one who loves you first. Welcome to your next level of intimacy in God; take these and use them to get to where you need to go in God. Are you ready? Let's go!

"Sing Unto God, Sing Praises To His Name"... Ps. 68:4

Setting the atmosphere for an encounter with God is very important in the life of a Christian. It's all about creating a relationship, not religion, with God. *Matthew 7: 22,23 says, "Many will in that day say to me that day, Lord, Lord, have we not prophesied in your name? and in your name cast out devils? And in your name cast out devils? and in thy name does many wonderful works? And then I will profess unto them, I never knew you depart from me ye that work iniquity."* So as you can see from this text that it's not about you serving and using your God-given gifts in church; He gives those out with no repentance (Romans 11:29), but it's all about cultivating your relationship with the one who is the actual head of the church.

Let me ask a couple of questions. Married couples, when you are setting up a moment of personal intimacy with your husband or wife, how would you do it? How would you set the tone? What kind of music would you play to get the atmosphere right for a sweet communion with the one you love? *I woke up with my mind stayed on Jesus?* Well, we know a church hymn will definitely spoil that mode; you'd probably pull out some of those good old-fashioned love songs from Luther Vandross or Kenny G to set the right mood for where you are attempting to go. Guess what? Setting the atmosphere for God should be set up the same way, to create an intimate moment with Him that will leave you thirsting and hungering for more of Him.

God wants to have tangible (touchable) moments with you daily. For that to happen, just like anything else, you have to take the time to make it happen intentionally. Music can play a big part in setting the tone for an encounter with God. I mentioned earlier that I am a musician who plays the piano & keyboard. Sometimes, I will sit down at my electric piano, close my eyes and begin to think about all He's done for me. I lose myself as I play a known praise and worship song and go into a free flow of prophetic music until I feel the Spirit of the Lord come into the room. During one of those times of intimacy, the Lord told me to go to the music studio and record an instrumental prayer music CD. Yes, God will talk to you and tell you what He wants you to do once you get into His presence.

I went on ahead and made an instrumental album back in 2018 called "Set Your Atmosphere," which is specifically for prayer time moments. Whenever you hear God prompting you to do something, do it. It might seem wild or have you going out of your personal comfort zone, but remember, you don't have to be a professional singer to sing to the Lord. God loves to hear us sing and give Him the thanksgiving and praises that He alone is due.

There is a song with a particular sound that the Lord wants to hear from you. This sound will create avenues of miracles, signs, and wonders in your home as you cultivate your relationship with God daily.

Let's be clear, you don't have to be a professional singer or be in a choir or praise team to sing to the Lord. Just make your joyful noise; it doesn't matter what you sound like to Him. If your praise is sincere, God will receive it and draw nigh to you (James 4:8).

I love to listen to anointed singers and musicians who flow in the spirit with their God-given gifts. LISTEN It's not enough for you to just have talented singers and musicians; it's the anointing, not the gifting that destroys the yokes of bondage. (Read Isaiah 10:27) This is another subject, y'all, but the right music recorded from someone who is in the right place in God can truly set the atmosphere for an authentic move IN God. Even during your private moments of intercession in your own home. The church building is not the only place you can have an encounter with God. The church is more than just a building; we ARE the church. So wherever we are, that's where He shows up if we allow Him to. Understand if you build up a place for Him to come, He will show up. God is Omnipresent; He's everywhere at the same time. He never forces Himself into a place where He is not wanted. You have to truly want Him and then literally welcome Him in to have His way. When you intentionally set up a place for the Lord to dwell with you, He will come and meet you right where you are at the point of your faith. Matthew 18:20 says, *"For where two or three are gathered together in my name, there am I in the midst of them."* Just as sure as He dwells with the two or three, know if it's you alone wanting to spend a private moment with Him, He will come. Read John 15:7. Ask God to guide you through the leading of the Holy Spirit to the right songs that will lead you into his presence. He'll do it. I'm a living witness to that.

Entering His Gates With Thanksgiving

Thanksgiving- The Expression of Gratitude Especially To God

The second step towards getting into the presence of God is through a sincere heart of thanksgiving. Psalms 100:4 says, *"Enter INTO His gates with thanksgiving...."* There is more to this verse, but we will stop here; a lot of times, we bypass this part because we want to cut across the yard and get to the place of giving God our "Christmas Wish List." Not saying that it's not good to ask Him for things, but the Bible says in Matthew 7:7, "Ask and it shall be given to you...' I'm just saying don't let that be the only reason to talk to Him. How would you feel if people only talked to you because they wanted something? God desires to have a real relationship with us. It is outlined plainly how to start that right here in this verse. *"Enter into His gates (a point of entry) with thanksgiving, AND into HIS Courts with PRAISE, Be THANKFUL unto Him AND bless His Name (Psalms 100:4.) This verse speaks about two different points of entry that will guide you to God. The scripture said to, "Enter into His gates with thanksgiving...." Is* the gate on the inside or the outside of the place where God is? I'm pretty sure you have already answered it's on the OUTSIDE. The outer court is just that. The *outer court* this actually means we haven't entered into His presence yet, so how do we get into His gates? By the giving of thanks. How do we start that process?

You thank God for *EVERYTHING:* for waking you up, for health and strength, for a place to live, for a job if you have one or a business, for His power of protection and provision, for His love and mercy and grace, for Jesus, and the Holy Spirit. When you are thanking God from a sincere heart, it will open up the door for you to praise Him from a sincere place. Knowing how to get into the presence of God will catapult you into an encounter with Him you will never forget, leaving you hungering and thirsting for more of Him

Entering His Courts With Praise/ Singing Your Song to the Lord

Psalms 100:4 says, *"Enter into his courts with praise..."* Praise, what is that? The original definition from the dictionary says, "Express warm approval or admiration of." What is Admiration? *"Respect and warm approval."* This word comes from the root word *"Admire"* to regard with wonder or approval. God desires praise from us. It is the actual giving of accolades and compliments. Praise is so important that it has been mandated for everything that has breath to do it in Psalms 150.

Here are some examples of praise;

You're a Good God. You're an awesome Father.
You are a wonderful and amazing God.
There's no God like You. You are great and greatly to be praised.
Lord, You are beautiful in every way; you are magnificent in all of your ways.

Let me put it like this: When someone says, "Hey, you did an awesome job dealing with that complaining customer today." Or "You are looking absolutely stunning and beautiful," Or "I saw you pay for that person's groceries at the store that you didn't even know; you're a great person!" How does it make you feel? Proud? Uplifted? Wanted, special? All of the above? Just like we all need to be edified, God wants to be glorified.

These are all example statements of praise and adoration which are designed to maneuver God into feeling loved or valued by us as His people. This is what God desires from us daily. One thing I know is that God loves to be praised. I believe I can even go so far as to say He loves to be sung to. Otherwise, Psalms 96:1-2 wouldn't tell us to *"Sing to the Lord a <u>new</u> song, Sing to the Lord praise His name; proclaim His salvation day after day…* verse 13 of the same chapter says, *"They will sing before the Lord, for he comes, he comes to judge the earth. He will judge the world in righteousness and the peoples in His truth."*

Start living a life of praise before Him regularly. When you do, it opens the door of intimacy with God, and that's when your personal walk with him begins. God desires to have a relationship with you, and the key to that is quality time spent with him. Get to the place where, as soon as you call, He will answer. Read Psalms 145:18; as we go through the praise scriptures, make it personal between you and God. Talk to Him as you meditate on these scriptures, say them aloud to Him, and mean them when you say them. Watch God begin to move in your life because you have availed yourself to learning how to be a true authentic praiser of the Most High God. You will be a part of the elite who know how to *"…worship Him in SPIRIT AND in truth"*. John 4:24

What's worship, you may ask? By definition, it means to lay down prostrate to bow oneself down in homage to another physically. Worship is a place in God where the miraculous happens. It's a place of total submission to God. It's a place of true intimacy where He embraces you, and you can embrace Him back through a totally surrendered heart. It's a wonderful place to be in God and is definitely attainable if you mean business and are in true pursuit of God. As you read the scriptures in this book, make them your words between you and the Father. What a way to cultivate your relationship with God through the use of His Words. Welcome to the wonderful world of giving God praise through the scriptures!

Let's Enter His Gates Together...

Psalms 100:4 *"Enter His gates with thanksgiving and His courts with praise, give thanks to Him and bless His Name."*

Psalms 7:17 *"I will give the Lord the thanks due to His righteousness ...*

Psalms 9:1 *"I will give thanks to You, LORD, with all my heart: I will tell of all your wonderful deeds."*

Psalms 35:18 *"I will give thanks in the great congregation I will praise thee among the people."*

Psalms 50:14 *"Sacrifice thank offerings to God, fulfill your vows to the LORD.*

Psalms 69:30 *"I will praise God's name in song and glorify him with thanksgiving.*

Psalms 92:1 *"A Psalm (or) Song for the Sabbath Day. (It is a) good [thing] to give thanks unto the LORD and His strength, and His wonderful works that He has done."*

Psalms 95:2 *"Let us come before Him with thanksgiving and extol Him with music and song*

Psalms 106:1 *"Praise the LORD. Give thanks to the LORD, for He is good; His love endures forever*

Psalms 107:1 *"Oh give thanks unto the Lord for He is good, for His steadfast love endures forever!"*

Psalms 95:2 *"Let us come before Him with thanksgiving and extol Him with music and song*

Psalms 107:8 *"Let them give thanks to the Lord for His unfailing love and his wonderful deeds for mankind."*

Psalms 116:17 *"I will offer praise to thee the sacrifice of Thanksgiving and will call upon the name of the Lord."*

Psalms 136:26 *"Oh give thanks unto the God of heaven: for His mercy endures for ever."*

A truly thankful heart is a grateful heart that will lead you into true moment of praise. Here are some of the Names of God you can incorporate your personal times of prayer, praise and worship with God!

Abba- Father, Daddy

Jehovah Rohi- My Shepherd

Elohim- The Creator of Heaven and Earth

Jehovah Shammah- The Lord my Helper (always there)

El- Shaddai- The God of Almighty Blessings

El Elyon- The God Most High

El Olam- The Everlasting God

El Roi- The God who sees

Adonai- My Lord and Jehovah Rapha- My Healer

Jehovah-M' Kaddesh- The Lord my Sanctifier

Jehovah Nissi- My Banner

Jehovah Shalom- My Peace

Jehovah Tsidkenu- My Righteousness

TRACEY BASSETT-DAVIS

Let's Enter His Courts With Praise...

Psalms 9:1 "I will praise thee, O Lord with my whole heart, I will shew forth all thy marvelous works

Psalms 9:2 "I will be glad and rejoice in thee: I will sing praises to thy name, O thou most High."

Psalms 9:11 "Sing praises to the LORD, which dwellers in Zion; declare among the people His doings."

Psalms 16:2 "I say to the Lord, You are my Lord, apart from You I have no good thing.'

Psalms 22:3 "But thou (art) holy, (O thou) that inhabitest the praises of Israel."

Psalms 27:6 "And now shall mine head be lifted up above mine enemies round about me; therefore will I offer in His tabernacle" sacrifices of joy; I will sing, yea, I will sing praises unto the LORD."

Psalms 34:1 "I will bless the Lord at all times: His praises shall continually be in my mouth."

Psalms 42:1 "As the deer panteth after the water brooks, so panteth my soul after thee, O God."

Psalms 42: 2 "My soul thirsts for God, for the living God…"

Psalms 42:4&5 "When I remember these things, I pour out my soul in me. For I had gone with the multitude, I went with them to the House of God, with the voice of joy and praise, with a multitude that kept holyday ….For I shall praise him for the help of his countenance."

Psalms 42:11 "Who art thou cast down, O my soul? And why art thou disquieted within me? Hope thou in God; for I shall yet praise Him, who is the health of my countenance, and my God."

Psalms 47:6 "Sing praises to God, sing praises; sing praises unto our King, sing praises."

Psalms 47:7 "For God (is) the King of all the earth; sing ye praises with understanding"

Psalms 56:12 "Thy vows (are) upon me, O God; I will render praises unto thee".

Psalms 63:3-4 "Because thy lovingkindness is better than life, my lips shall praise thee. Thus will I bless thee while I live: I will lift up my hands in thy name."

Psalms 66:17 "I cried unto him with my mouth, and he was extolled with my tongue."

Psalms 68:4 "Sing unto God, sing praises to His name; extol Him that rideth upon the heavens by His name JAH, and rejoice before Him."

Psalms 68:32 "Sing unto God, ye kingdoms of the earth; O sing praises unto the Lord; Selah"

Psalms 71:8 "Let my mouth be filled with thy praise and with thy honour all the day."

Psalms 103: "Bless the Lord, O my soul: and all that is within me, bless His holy name."

Psalms 105: "Give praise to the Lord, proclaim His name; make known among the nations what He has done.

Psalms 108:3 "I will praise thee, O LORD, among the people; and I will sing praises unto thee among the nations."

Psalms 119:7 "I will praise thee with uprightness of heart, when I shall have learned thy righteous judgements."

Psalms 135:3 "Praise the LORD, for the LORD [is] good; sing praises unto His name; for [it is] pleasant."

Psalms 144:9 "I will sing a new sing unto thee, O God; upon a psaltery (and) an instrument of ten strings will I sing praises unto thee"

Psalms 145:1 "I will extol thee my God, O King; and I will bless thy name for ever and ever."

Psalms 145:2 "Everyday will I bless thee; and I will praise thy name for ever and ever."

Psalms 145:3 "Great is the Lord, and greatly to be praised; and His greatness is unsearchable."

Psalms 145:8 "The Lord is gracious, and full of compassion, slow to anger, and of great mercy."

Psalms 145:10,11 "All thy works shall Praise thee, O Lord; and thy saints shall bless thee. (11) They shall speak of the glory of thy kingdom, and talk of thy power."

Psalms 145:21 " My mouth shall speak the praise of the Lord; and let all flesh bless His holy name forever and ever."

Psalms 146:2 "While I live will I praise the LORD; I will sing praises unto my God while I have any being."

Psalms 147:1 "Praise ye the LORD; for (it is) good to sing praises unto our God; for (it is) please thank; (and) praise is comely."

Psalms 149:3 "Let them praise His name in the dance; let them sing praises unto Him with the timbre and harp."

Psalms 149:6 "(Let), the high (praises) of God (be) in their mouth, and a two-edged sword in their hand."

Psalms 150:1 " Praise ye the Lord. Praise God in His sanctuary; praise Him in the firmament of His power."

Psalms 150:2 "Praise Him for His mighty acts; praise Him according to His excellent greatness."

Psalms 150:3 "Praise Him with the sound of the trumpet; praise Him with the psaltery and harp."

Psalms 150:4 "Praise Him with the timbrel and dance; praise Him with the stringed instruments and organs."

More Gems To Help Worship Him In Spirit And Truth.

Isaiah 25:1 'Lord, You are my God, I will exalt (lift) and praise Your name, For in perfect faithfulness You have done wonderful things, things planned long ago."

1 Samuel 2:2 "There is no one holy like the Lord; there is no one besides You; there is no Rock like our God.

2 Samuel 7:22 "How great you are, Sovereign Lord! There is no one like you, and there is no God but you, as we have heard with our own ears."

1 Chronicles 29:11 "Yours Lord, is the greatness and the power and the glory and majesty and the splendor, for everything in heaven and earth is yours. Yours Lord is the kingdom you are exalted as head overall.'

Jeremiah 1:14 "Heal me O Lord, and I shall be healed; save me and I shall be saved; for thou art my praise."

You can take time to find even more scriptures to incorporate here and put them in the space below;

Conclusion

These scriptures are to be used during your personal times of prayer and other intimate times spent with God at home. As you read this book, make each step personal; that's the key to ministering to God correctly. A lot of times, people think that this type of thing is to just be done during a corporate setting at church by an intercessor, minister, pastor, evangelist, or anyone leading the congregation into what's normally done in the church setting.

No, the truth of the matter is entering into His gates with thanksgiving and into His courts with praise is a mandate for all of us, no matter where we are. Establishing a place for God to dwell in our daily walk with Him is something we should all be doing at the start of each new day we are blessed with. Why? Because it sets the tone for God to move in our lives each day. When the scene for communion with the Lord is set up properly first thing in the morning, and an authentic connection is made, it opens the door for whatever God has for you to be released, and it sets in order God's Plan for your life throughout that day.

Proverbs 3:6 says, *"In all your ways acknowledge Him, and He will direct your path."* this can only come into manifestation when you do this intentionally and daily. Remember, it's about establishing a *relationship* with God. It's all about giving Him what He rightfully deserves every day all day. Be obedient to what He tells you to do when He speaks, whether it be through Him speaking personally to you, through the Word of God, or through someone He sends. God uses different ways to speak to us; sometimes, it's even that "still small voice" that we always call "Something." God talks to all of us, but those that are His, follow His Voice only and no one can take them out of His Hand (John 10: 27-28.)

Our main goal is to get into His presence daily; after all, how can you tap in and be beckoned to come behind the veil into the Holy of Holies where He is, if you haven't entered the gate and the court areas mentioned in the book of Psalms? In order to get into His presence, these things have to be done on a regular basis. Just like time is carved out intentionally for people who are significant to you, that same intention needs to be there for God.

Don't try to get into His presence because of what He can do for you. You won't be able to get there that way. Only the pure in heart shall see God. Only true worshippers can get into His presence. God knows your heart when you come before Him, so be real. If your heart is not right and you have ulterior motives, He sees and knows already. Come clean and if you are not saved, get saved today. If you are unsaved and you would like to give your life over to God right now, repeat these words:

> *"Lord, I am a sinner. I have done wrong and am asking for you to forgive me of all my sins and wash me clean from all unrighteousness. I believe that Jesus is the Son of God and that You sent Him here to earth to be born, live, and die for my sins on the cross at Calvary. I believe He has risen from the dead and is now seated at Your right hand. King Jesus I accept you as my personal Savior; please come into my heart and save me now, receive me into your Kingdom. I openly receive the Gift of the Holy Spirit that has been offered to me freely. Like on the Day of Pentecost they waited for the promise of you to come and fill them, I don't have to tarry like they did back then, all I have to do is claim and receive the gift by faith that has been given to me. So now I ask in Jesus Name, Holy Spirit come I receive you by faith and welcome you to take over. I ask for you to baptize me with fire and stir up the heavenly language within my belly that serves as proof of your living on the inside of me. Have your way, break every chain, destroy all yokes of bondage in my life. Thank you for helping me to grow and mature in the ways of you and for allowing me to grow from faith to faith and glory to glory. Old things are passed away; behold all things are now new! I am now a new creature in You. Thank you for welcoming me into your kingdom. Keep me sealed until the time of redemption in Jesus Name Amen."*

If you are a backslider know that God still loves you and is patiently waiting for you to return back to Him now is the time, let's do it now repeat after me:

"Lord, I'm coming before you now as a backslider I have sinned against you and have turned from the faith to live a life outside of the will you had purposed for my life. Today, I repent from all of my sins and rededicate myself to you today please give me a clean heart, renew the right spirit within me and cleanse me from all unrighteousness, deliver me from the hand of Satan and his minions I, denounce and renounce all sin in my life that has easily beset me and I totally surrender my all to you. Holy Spirit fall afresh on me stir up every gift on the inside of me, if I have never received the Baptism of the Holy Spirit with the evidence of speaking in tongues. I call upon you now Holy Spirit to take me over you are the part of the Holy Trinity that is here now to lead, guide and direct me to all truth so I surrender to you Holy Spirit saturate me through and through burn away everything that's not like you. I give you full reign in my life. Thank you for receiving me back into the Kingdom this day in Jesus Name, amen!"

If you repeated either prayer welcome to the Family of God, you are a new creature in Him whether you are receiving Jesus for the first time or have rededicated yourself. Congratulations, now your new life in Christ can begin. Those of you who are in God and want to get closer to Him, dig right in, follow the directions of this book, and you will have great success. Those of you who have just rededicated and received Jesus for the first time, find a fivefold ministry where you can grow. Ask God; he will direct you to the right place to go if you let Him. Start your walk with the Lord today don't wait.

I'm here to tell you I am a living witness concerning the goodness of God. He will transform your spirit and renew your mind. Release yourself to Him fully. Let His desires become your desires. Get before Him because you desire to *be* with Him and you love Him, not because of what He can give you. When you get caught up in the Creator and not the Creator's Stuff, everything you could ever need, want, or desire will automatically follow because you chose to abide in Him daily. Surrender to God, spend intimate time with Him, be obedient to what He tells you, and let the process be the process. Trust Him, and not only will you have great success in life, but you will have what's even more important; a fantastic relationship with God that will leave you in total awe and adoration concerning who He is. Now go and use your "Psalms In The Sand."

About The Author

Tracey Bassett-Davis is the youngest daughter of Ernest and Lucy Bassett, a Chicago Native who grew up in the Northwest Indiana area. The youngest of three siblings, Vanessa and Ollie Bassett. Her mother, Lucy, passed away in November 2020 due to contracting COVID-19 in a physical rehabilitation facility and is now taking care of her elderly father, Ernest Bassett. Tracey is the CEO and founder of Born 2 Worship Him LLC. She is an accomplished Minstrel, Psalmist, Songwriter, Praise and Worship Leader, and Instructor who has sung, trained, and accompanied many soloists, recording and local church choirs, and singing groups and has led worship services throughout the Northwest Indiana, Greater Chicagoland area and the United States. She has also participated as a vocal instructor for a gospel music conference in Los Angeles, California.

Tracey was a SCAP Spiritual Care Associate Provider for Gary Methodist Hospital South and Northlake Campuses. She has an Associates Degree in Business Management (2017). Tracey is about to graduate in May of 2022 with another Associates Degree, this time in Early Childhood Development, with over 20 years of experience. She is a minister and the Intercessory Prayer Ministry Leader and praise team leader at the church she attends, along with her husband of 20 years this December of 2021. Her husband, Pastor Mark Davis, is the Outreach Pastor for Life Church International located in Gary, Indiana, where her Senior Pastors are Roosevelt and Lady LaFonda Bradley. Tracey is a mother of 5 beautiful children, 2 of those through marriage Christine, Jeremy, Devon, Mark Jr., and Naomi. Tracey and her Husband Mark have just joined the *"Empty*

Nest Club "(No more kids in the house, just sent the last baby off to college). She is also a loving grandmother of five beautiful grandchildren Dion, Chris, Carley, Mark III, and Morgan. Above all else, she is a lover of The Most High God and has claimed herself to be a passionate worshipper at heart and is quick to give God all the glory, honor, and praise in every season of life. She desires that this book be used as a point of contact for God to move in the lives of every reader and teach others how to get into the Presence of God themselves so true change can occur in the lives of all touched by this reading.

> For Bookings, contact Minister Tracey at
> born2worshiphimenterprises@gmail.com

www.ingramcontent.com/pod-product-compliance
Lightning Source LLC
Chambersburg PA
CBHW051713090426
42736CB00013B/2691